First published in December 2021

Further copies and fundraising information from Jules Sherwood
(jules.sherwood@stclementdanesraf.org)
St Clement Danes Church Fund
Registered Charity No 1168717

Design by Adrian Wood

Printed by DLM Limited

One of the most prestigious church organs in London

St Clement Danes Church dates back over a thousand years, to the very origins of England as a nation state.

Our Books of Remembrance commemorate by name over 150,000 people who have lost their lives whilst serving in the RAF.

St Clement Danes Church

For more than a thousand years, there has been a place of worship at the end of the Strand, just yards from the western boundary of the City of London and the Royal Courts of Justice. The church of St Clement Danes is so named for the patron saint of mariners, chosen by the Danes after promising King Alfred the Great to build a place of Christian worship.

The current church was designed and built under the guidance of Sir Christopher Wren and completed in 1682. During the construction, the crypt was filled, burying 500 years of presumed Danish tombs. The church was gutted by fire bombs in the Blitz of 1941, rebuilt and by 1958 had been re-consecrated as a perpetual shrine of remembrance to those who have died in service in the Royal Air Force.

The Crypt

St Clement Danes has one of the most prestigious church organs in London and a beautifully maintained set of working bells. They peel the famous 'oranges and lemons' from the traditional nursery rhyme throughout the day. It is a living church prayed in and visited throughout the year by thousands of people seeking solace and reflection.

It is fitting then to celebrate this national treasure with a distinctive cocktail and a tailored martini, both of which bring geography, history and delight in equal measures.

St Clement Danes
Cocktail Collection

This Collection of Cocktails started as a simple idea to create an appropriate cocktail to celebrate St Clement Danes Church and all it means to the Royal Air Force and the local community. A second cocktail was envisaged for non-gin drinkers (there are some, apparently) and then the light bulb went on – of course, a Collection. So a simple exercise was started: find appropriate cocktails with appropriate Royal Air Force meanings. Simple? Actually, yes, and with the help of some fellow cocktail advocates and members of No 601 (County of London) Squadron, a joy.

The next stage was to ensure that the project for a book of collected cocktails fell within the aims and ambitions of the fund-raising team led by Jules Sherwood. They were immediately enthusiastic and ready to contribute. The key is not just to collect interesting cocktails but to raise money for a very worthwhile cause. The designer Adrian Wood has been a clairvoyant in translating the raw material into an excellent publication of which we are all justly proud.

We all opened our black books, and the result is a most interesting collection of sponsors and cocktails. A special call-out goes to devisers, planners, mixers and tasters: Honorary Group Captain Sally Bridgeland, Eloise Coombs and Squadron Leader Emilie Long.

Finally, the Appeal and the author are indebted to Air Chief Marshal Sir Mike Wigston, the Chief of the Air Staff for both his support and the offering up of a Margarita which it might be suggested that every upwardly mobile Station Commander has available.

Paul Beaver

Paul Beaver

Sally Bridgeland

Eloise Coombs

Foreword

I was delighted to be asked to write the foreword for this wonderful collection of cocktails generously compiled by connoisseur Hon. Group Captain Paul Beaver No 601 (County of London) Squadron RAuxAF, in support of the 1941 Appeal for St Clement Danes Church, the central church of the Royal Air Force.

Each cocktail has a Royal Air Force theme from the past, present and future and I hope you will find time to enjoy and truly savour these special recipes.

I wish to thank all our sponsors and friends of the Royal Air Force and St Clement Danes who have made this book possible and of course a special thanks to Paul for developing the recipes.

By purchasing this book, you are supporting the future of St Clement Danes. The 1941 Appeal aims to raise £10m which will secure our central church of the Royal Air Force as a place of remembrance and reflection for future generations.

If you would like to support the 1941 Appeal even further, you will find details on our website:

https://stclementdanesraf.org/1941-2021/

I hope you enjoy creating your St Clement Danes Cocktails, and will raise your glass in honour of those who gave their all for our freedom, and are forever remembered in our church.

Thank you.

Air Chief Marshal
Sir Mike Wigston KCB CBE ADC
Chief of the Air Staff

A Word About Cocktails

Cocktails may have been invented in America at the turn of the 19th century, but the British have taken them to heart too. Why? It's simple – we have the best gin, whisky/whiskey in the world and even our vodka passes the test. Soon, thanks to climate change, we'll have outstanding sparkling wine and even vermouth, that staple of a good martini, made in London. James Bond made the Vesper famous, but it was his author Ian Fleming who first devised it in Duke's Hotel, Mayfair – here in London.

But what makes a good cocktail? Besides a good mixologist, it is a matter of personal choice. I like a gin martini to start a meal; a French 75 is the summer choice; perhaps a negroni for the winter. My main collaborator has other choices: Eloise preferring whisky neat and spiced Russian vodka to create her cocktails. She has also been known to accept a French 75, modified to her exacting taste buds, of course.

Creating this book, we have been blessed with supporters contributing ideas and then allowing the team to subtly manipulate the flavours using the right measures and the right supporting bitters or herbs. The key is to get the base right. Then, remember not to add too much ice, so as not to dilute the cocktail. Most benefit for stirring but other can be shaken – James Bond's Vesper is certainly better stirred not shaken – I know, it's running against the grain but, trust me…….

And one last thought – history records that a gallant American general named a drink which settled a battle after the vanquished commander's daughter. She was called Coctel and that was quickly corrupted to Cocktail.

Paul (Pablo) Beaver
Honorary Group Captain
No 601 (County of London) Squadron

Standing together for Ukraine

During the preparation of this second edition to the **St Clement Danes Cocktail Collection**, the Russian Federation lunched an unprovoked attack on Ukraine. Members of No 601 Squadron, supporting the **1941 Appeal** thought it was important to show solidarity with the Ukrainian people and their flag. It reminded us of the brave Americans who saw what Hitler was doing in Europe and came to Britain's aid in 1940.

Several experiments were made at London's RAF Club to create the **Ukrainian Flag Cocktail** – variously called the *Resistance* or a *Still Standing* as suggested by Dr Jenny Johnson. It consists of equal measures of the velvety yellow Warninks Advocaat and the sweet De Kuyper Blue Curaçao. The trick is to get the mixture to layer and so a little egg white mixed with the advocaat will do the trick. The glass should be cold and held steady during the preparation. Take care when drinking, it's lethal, just like the Ukrainian patriots.

Another use for curaçao is to mix it with champagne for a delightful blue cocktail and perhaps cut it with a few drops of Angostura orange bitters. No name yet but perhaps *Sally Further!* might be appropriate.

Picture © John Goodman

St Clement Danes Cocktail

It has to be 'oranges and lemons' for this London Dry Gin cocktail. London Gin is pure and bursting with juniper. When added to the juice of fresh citrus and the tang of the Fiero liquor and Aquavit for the Danish connection - it's a memorable stunner.

Ingredients

City of London Dry Gin
Aalborg Danish Aquavit
Martini & Rosso Fiero
Fresh oranges and lemons

Method

Fill a shaker with ice
Add three parts Fiero; one part gin; half part aquavit
Make up, to taste, with the juice of freshly squeezed citrus – Amalfi lemons and Outspan oranges
Swirl, never shake, strain and serve
And keep serving as long as there is a Royal Air Force

Kindly sponsored by

City Hive is working to build an inclusive Investment Management Industry and an equitable and sustainable society.

St Clement Danes Martini

For 100 years, we've been embracing change, innovating and navigating uncertainty. Working alongside employers, trustees and financial services institutions Hymans Robertson offers independent pensions, investments, benefits and risk consulting services with a friendly, straightforward and partnering approach to everything we do.

We are passionate about building long term sustainable futures for Charities through financial and ethical promises to both charitable projects and employees. We recognise the challenges charities face are very different dependent on their needs.

The ultimate London Martini has to be this one crafted from City of London gin, Londinio nine-botanicals vermouth and Danish aquavit

Ingredients

City of London Dry Gin
Aalborg Danish Aquavit
Londinio Vermouth
Angostura orange bitters
Ice

Method

Fill a shaker with ice – add the vermouth
add three parts gin; half part aquavit;
add two splashes of bitters
swirl, never shake, strain and serve
Keep drinking in memory of those who served before
us and liked their martini stirred and not shaken

Pablo's Margarita

For more than 100 years, the Royal Air Force has been the leader in diverse and inclusive military thinking. It thrives on different leadership styles, exemplified by a long line of Chiefs who see change and innovation as true marks of leadership.

This cocktail has been created to honour the Chiefs of Air Staff since Lord Trenchard in 1918.

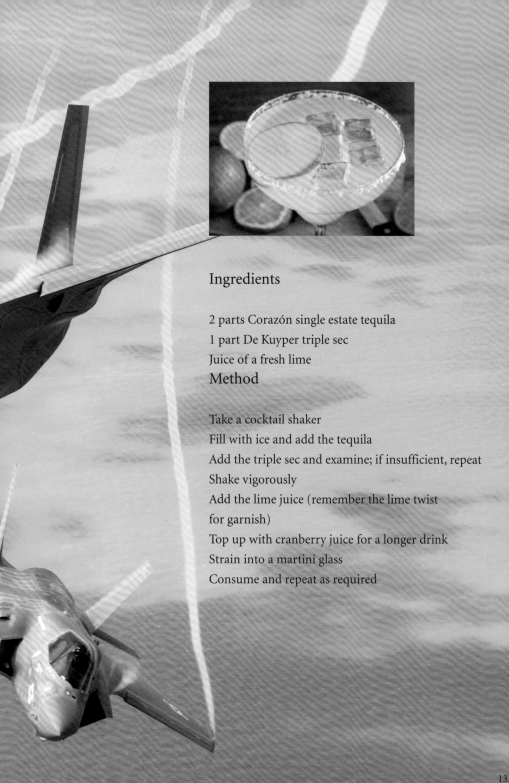

Ingredients

2 parts Corazón single estate tequila
1 part De Kuyper triple sec
Juice of a fresh lime

Method

Take a cocktail shaker
Fill with ice and add the tequila
Add the triple sec and examine; if insufficient, repeat
Shake vigorously
Add the lime juice (remember the lime twist
for garnish)
Top up with cranberry juice for a longer drink
Strain into a martini glass
Consume and repeat as required

Flying Sword

No 601 (County of London) Squadron

Group Captain Guy Austin writes: I have regretful memories of the morning after what seemed like a good idea the night before in a bar in South Africa. Why red drinks seemed like a good idea I have no idea, I also have a vague memory that flaming Lamborghinis were involved, amongst other concoctions. This one was Martini Rosso and a delicious vodka. And there was something else.

Work the next day was "difficult" but I know I made it, though it felt as if someone had thrust a sword into my head for sure. Perfect for 601!

Paracetamol couldn't touch the headache.

Kindly sponsored by GA1956 Ltd

Supermarine Spitfire Mk.Vc, BP955, 'J.1' flown by
Flt. Lt. Denis Barnham of 601 Squadron, Royal Air Force,
based at Luqa, Malta, April, 1942.

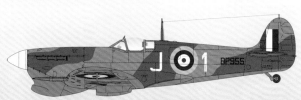

Ingredients

2 parts vodka
3 parts Martini & Rossi Rosso

As an additional kick
Klipdrift Premium Brandy is distilled in vintage copper
pot stills and then sealed in the finest French oak and
left for time and the angels.

French 75 (mod)

Rocket fuel for the Royal Flying Corps

In 1914, the Royal Flying Corps self-deployed with their aeroplanes from Britain to France in the first such military endeavour ever. All went well, until Lord Flashheart and his men discovered there was no tonic for the copious London gin with which they had been issued. Instead, the French Army provided something better, champagne! It was mixed in varying proportions until the ideal nectar was created. It was called a French 75 after the redoubtable artillery piece. Later, triple sec was added for a special kick and later still, in 2021, the addition of a single maraschino cherry created the ultimate summer cocktail and it seemed only right to amend the name, slightly.

Kindly sponsored by
Group Captain Paul & Mrs Fanette Newman

Tried and tested by Eloise Coombs

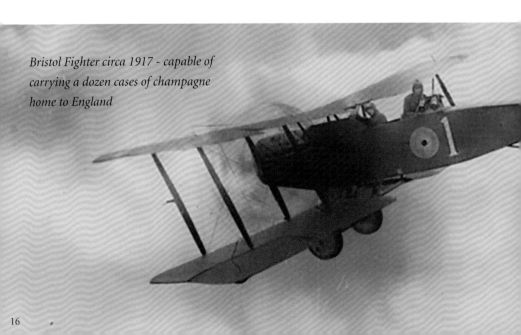

Bristol Fighter circa 1917 - capable of carrying a dozen cases of champagne home to England

Ingredients
Take a champagne flute and add

3 parts London gin
1 part Cointreau triple sec
A single Maraschino cocktail cherry
As much Champagne as needed
(but never Prosecco)

SIDE BY SIDE ~
BRITANNIA

The Special Relationship

Cup of English Breakfast tea (hot or cold)
1 shot of fresh California lemon juice
(Amalfi if in Europe)
1 shot of honey syrup
(depending of required sweetness)
1 shot King's Ginger
4 shots American Dry Gin
8 dashes Angostura bitters.

For the hot just pour it all into a jug and stir
For cold put into a jug full with ice and stir

Kindly sponsored by the Billy Fiske Foundation

Actuary's Angel

Sally B, today preserved in England, was one of the last Boeing B-17 Flying Fortress bombers to be built, accepted in June 1945 but then converted for training then for survey work. She survived the Second World War unlike many thousands of young American aircrew who perished on perilous daylight missions over Occupied Europe and Germany. We salute those who flew up to Heaven on an angel's wing.

Ingredients

1 part white crème de cacao
1 part French brandy
1 part half-and-half cream

Method

Mix together in a highball glass, stirring carefully so as to not separate the ingredients. Raise your glass to Heaven and remember the brave.

*The first three lady Masters of the Worshipful Company of Actuaries are delighted to sponsor this angelic concoction which also celebrates the affiliation with No 601 Sqn initiated by the first lady Master when the Squadron reformed in 2017.

*Sally B, Fiona M and Julie G

WORSHIPFUL COMPANY
OF
ACTUARIES

Forces Mutual Mojito

When the going gets tough, we've got your back. With almost 30 years experience across the military, we understand the financial side of Air Force life. We offer a range of products and services specific to the military. We are your financial ally.

Mojito is a fine cocktail - who could forget James Bond standing on a beach in the West Indies sipping a fresh-made mojito, brimming with fresh mint. He pretends to bird-watch when he was actually watching a bikini-clad 'bird'. The key to a good mojito is the rum. Down in Barbados, they distil a fine heritage rum which is pale gold and mixes so well with lime and mint. The Mount Gay Eclipse is the rum of choice for a sound mojito.

It is best made in a jug to share. Fill the jug with mint, add three limes, a tablespoon of sugar syrup – muddle fiercely – add ice and rum. Top up with soda water (one can always add more but never subtract so take care). Pour into a tall glass and find a comfortable seat to consume, watching the frigate birds if one is lucky enough to be on the Equator.

Ingredients

2 parts Mount Gay Eclipse Heritage rum
Sugar syrup
(home made is preferrable)
Fresh mint
At least 3 limes
Ice and soda water

The Flaming Hot

Like hitting the reheat on a QRA Typhoon

In times when I'm host to the blasted, throat-scratching, nasal-clogging bug that is(wo)man flu, I know the element I need is not earth, wind, Vicks or water, but fire. That is, the fire that can be found in the unadulterated, soul-warming heat of the Flaming Hot.

Inspired by the beloved and dependable "Hot Toddy", soother of the Common Cold, the Flaming Hot comes into its own when the hardiest of us require a little extra heat to really invigorate our senses. For those of us in full health, this serves as a drink with an enlivening peppery kick and a lasting smouldering warmth, to accompany any a cold winter's evening.

For one serving, simply grab your favourite heatproof glass (or mug if you are really ill) and add the whisky. I prefer a Scottish unpeated for this, but a whiskey will work too. You will then want to add 3 measures of freshly squeezed grapefruit juice, and 1 measure of ginger syrup into your chalice of choice. Finally, add in the two cloves and a generous pinch of cayenne pepper, and pour on 3 measures of boiling water. Stir, drink and relax into the fiery comfort that is the flaming hot.

By Eloise Coombs
whose cold was cured.

Kindly sponsored by
Haven Green Capital Partners

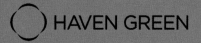

Ingredients

3 measures of Whisky, or Whiskey of your choosing. No need to use up your finest.

3 measures of grapefruit juice- freshly squeezed, ideally.

1 measure of Opie's stem ginger syrup, sweet enough to not require any added honey or sugar

2 whole cloves

1 generous pinch of cayenne pepper, to taste

3 measures boiling water

No 601 Squadron
Champagne Cocktail

Ingredients

3 parts Champagne brut
(in an emergency, Crémant de Loire is a possible
substitute but never Prosecco)
1 part Calvados Pays d'Auge Vieux
1 part orange juice
4 drops of Angostura bitters

Method

Into a Champagne flute
Add the bitters, swirl
Add the Champagne
Add the Calvados
Top up with orange juice, if required

Serve as often as needed

No 601 (County of London) Squadron has an enviable reputation. Born out
of the aspirations of three young men in search of adventure, it quickly became
a highly proficient Auxiliary Air Force unit which won bombing trophies in
the face of Regular competition. Just before the outbreak of the Second World War,
it became a fighter squadron, which it remained until 1957.

During the Battle of Britain, with its Hawker Hurricanes based at RAF Tangmere on the
Sussex coast, it bore the brunt of early fighting over the Channel and suffered casualties,
including American legend, Billy Fiske. It later flew Spitfires in the Mediterranean,
North Africa and Italy and, after the war, early jets in the air defence of Great Britain.

The Squadron was re-formed in 2017 to provide advice and new thinking to the Senior
Leadership Team of the Royal Air Force, including professional standards, sustainability,
and advocacy.

Battle of Britain Memorial Flight (BBMF) flypast of Spitfire (P7350) and Hurricane (PZ865).

The Investor's Return

Risk and reward. Hugh Dowding knew the risks were high in the Battle of Britain but he calculated the risks and won the reward that justified those risks. Dowding was, of course, the architect of the victory of the Battle of Britain in 1940.

Through his leadership in measuring the risks when he created the Dowding System – the world's first integrated air defence system – he knew how to use his scarce resource well and his investment in time and effort paid off. Through his leadership of Royal Air Force Fighter Command in 1940, the Nation was able to stem the threat of invasion and win the Battle of Britain.

Well researched investments deliver long term rewards.

Ingredients

Brown sugar cube soaked in
Angostura orange bitters
2 measures x Chateau de Lacquy
2004 Bas Armagnac
Top up with champagne

Kindly sponsored by

GUILD OF INVESTMENT MANAGERS

Black Buck Gin Martini

The Black Buck Raids

After the Argentine invasion of the Falkland Islands in 1982, Prime Minister Margaret Thatcher ordered the Crown dependency to be liberated. Part of the Royal Air Force contribution was a series of seven raids at extremely long-range by Vulcan bombers, supported by Victor tankers. The longest bombing raid in history is celebrated in the Black Buck Gin Martini, drunk in honour of the men and women who made it possible.

Ingredients

Wild Ram London Gin
Londinio London Vermouth
Fee Brothers' Black Walnut Bitters

Method

Take a cocktail shaker
Fill with ice and add four drops of bitters
Add one part of the vermouth
And swirl (do not shake)
Add three parts of gin
Swirl again – taking care not to cloud the vermouth
Pour into a cocktail glass
Raise a cheer and give thanks for the courage of the crews

Kindly
sponsored by

Champagne Claudia

The mighty Handley-Page Halifax bomber bore the brunt of the bomber offensive against Germany and Occupied Europe in the early years of the Second World War. Although slower and unable to fly as high as the Lancaster, it was beloved of its crews because, in an emergency, the crew had readily available escape hatches. One who escaped was Frank Stormont of No 192 Squadron in No 100 Group, the specialist electronic warfare unit. He took to the silk over Mailly-le-Camp, near Troyes in the Champagne Region after assaulting the pre- D-Day Panzer concentration. Frank survived the jump, evaded the Germans and was rescued by Claudia Bertain, a local champenois with a record of gallant help to downed aircrew. This champagne cocktail commemorates those brave people of No 100 Group but especially the gallant members of a French resistance circuit which protected Frank and so many downed aircrew.

Kindly sponsored by Frank's grandson Oliver Reeve and his wife Charlotte.
Oliver Reeve & Partners Limited
Partner Practice of St. James's Place Wealth Management

Ingredients

Champagne
A pinch of saffron
(Frank's burial place)
2 jiggers City of London gin
2 dashes Angostura orange bitters

Method

Take a tall flute; add two jiggers of
City of London gin
Add two dashes of orange bitters
Top up with Champagne – for extra
sweetness, a sugar cube can be added

The Old-Fashioned – full of charm and understated

This is a cocktail for the discerning palate. The base can be varied for the spirit available but the unmistakeable sweet-sour combination will make it outstanding with Canadian rye whiskey. To make a good old-fashioned, care needs to be taken and just as 'old-fashioned' is a much misunderstood term, so the cocktail needs to be taken seriously. For the full experience, add a twist of lemon as "oranges and lemons say the bells of St Clements".

Kindly sponsored by William Charnley

Ingredients

Canadian Club rye whiskey
Angostura orange bitters
Fresh orange juice
A single brown sugar cube

Method

Take a cocktail shaker; add the sugar lump
Add the fresh orange juice and two dashes of orange bitters
Overfill with ice and add two jiggers of Canadian Club rye whiskey, garnish with orange peel
Shake, strain and pour into a highball glass – after three of these cocktails, one is fluent in seven foreign languages but not English

St Clement Old Fashioned

Rigby Pathfinder

Don Bennett and the Pathfinders

Taking the Bomber Stream to its targets in the Big City (Berlin) or Happy Valley (the Ruhr) was the job of No 8 Group in RAF Bomber Command. Using the latest technology, the Group, led by the charismatic Air Marshal Don Bennett found and marked the targets to ensure accurate bombing. Bennett was the expert at long-range navigation and technical aviation who won awards and a place in aeronautical history. This take on the Tom Collins cocktail is a tribute to him and the men who served with him in the Second World War.

RAF reconnaisance photos of Berlin Tempelhof airport, Germany, in 1941, showing military aircraft on the runway apron

Ingredients

City of London gin
Angostura orange bitters
Caster sugar syrup

Method

Take a cocktail shaker; fill with ice and add two jiggers of City of London gin
Add two dashes of orange bitters and sugar syrup, stir gently
Pour into a highball glass – after three of these cocktails, try to find your way home

Kindly sponsored by Sir Peter Rigby, an industrial pathfinder in IT and aviation

Hitomi Blitz

It may have brought down the Church but we have re-built it

London and other cities in the United Kingdom were bombed nightly for several months from September 1940. London was hit the hardest but endured. Amongst the treasures which were hit and then rebuilt was the church of St Clement Danes. Today, we remember those events when we sample The Blitz, remembering that many cities were bombed from the air in the Second World War, including Belfast, Cardiff, Glasgow and Liverpool. The lives of so many were affected.

Ingredients

35 cl malt, blended whisky
Juice of a fresh lemon
A stick of cinnamon
Honey to taste
Boiling water

Method

First take an Amalfi lemon and curve a horse's neck of peel; then squeeze the entire fruit. Put on the kettle. Select your No 3 favourite whisky and some local honey. Raid the spice cabinet for cinnamon. Add everything into saucepan for ease when the boiling water is added. Allow to stand before consuming on a winter's day.

Kindly sponsored by HGC Andy Palmer

The Catalina Cocktail

It found the *Bismarck*, sank enemy submarines, rescued downed aircrew and achieved feats of maritime aviation close to miraculous. The Consolidated Catalina was one of the first 'buys' of the Anglo-American Lend-Lease arrangement which allowed Britain to fight on alone in Europe in 1940. Strong, with long range and the capability of landing on land as well as the sea, the Catalina remains a great example of the aeroplane builder's art. The Catalina Cocktail celebrates its widespread service, especially in support of the Royal Navy.

Ingredients

Navy Rum
Orange curaçao
Fresh lime juice
Fresh orange juice

Method

Take a cocktail shaker
Fill with ice and add two
jiggers of navy rum
Add the orange curaçao
Shake vigorously
Add one part lime juice to
two parts orange juice
Pour into a highball glass

Defiant

The *Luftwaffe* squadron leader could hardly believe their luck over Dunkirk that 28th May morning. A tight formation of British single-engined fighters from No 264 Squadron that had just taken off from RAF Manston on the Kent coast. He had 30 fighters – they were just ten – sitting duck? Well, no, actually, these fighters were Defiant turret fighters. The ten British aircraft forming a circle, and claimed six German fighters for the loss of three Defiants. The following day, the squadron claimed 19 Stuka dive-bombers but their luck couldn't last. The Germans learned quickly and found the Defiant vulnerable when attacked from below and the front – its only armament were machine guns in a turret. As a night fighter, it was different. The defiant claimed more German bombers in the night blitz than any other defence. Worth saying cheers to the gallant crews.

2 parts Guinness
1 part coca cola
1 part brandy

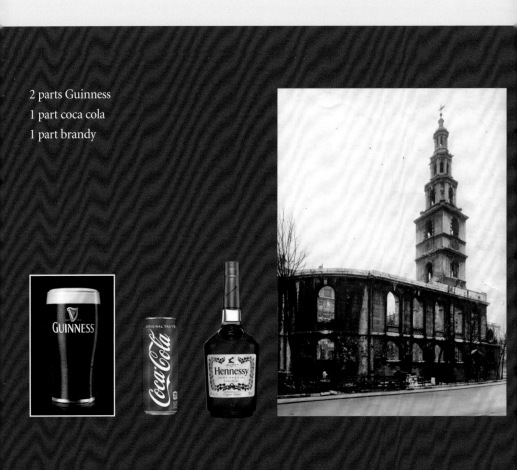

Bruce Dickinson writes:
"Rubbish as a day fighter but
good to down a few after dark...
I should know as I've downed
a few this year"

Blue & White

The blue and white colours represent the colours on the
Squadron Crest for Northumbrian Universities Air
Squadron – which draws from the Universities in the
North East of England with a Flying HQ at RAF Leeming
and a Town HQ near St Cuthbert's Keep in Newcastle.

The UAS across the country often provide the first taste of
the Royal Air Force for many and have been an entry to
the Service for some exceptional pilots and ground
branch individuals. The NUAS motto is 'Knowledge
Gives Wings'.

Only those on the Squadron will know the song which
accompanies the drinking of a 'blue and white' – and it
perhaps best that it remains that way!

Ingredients

Equal portions of the
following liqueurs

Baileys Irish Cream
Blue curaçao

Method

Add to a high ball glass
and allow to stand

Lethality at 50 paces

The Beamish

RAF Fighter Command was blessed with nearly a dozen Irish volunteers during the Battle of Britain and many more joined later.

There were also those who had come across the Irish Sea in the 1920s and 1930s, to serve with the Royal Air Force. Amongst those was Victor Beamish from County Cork. He commanded RAF North Weald and flew more than a hundred missions during the Battle, being decorated for gallantry three times.

Ingredients

Take a pint of Beamish stout and add two shots of Jameson whiskey from Cork.

W3649 became the personal aircraft of Group Captain Victor Beamish, DSO, DFC, and carried the code FV-B. He was reported missing over the Channel on 28th March 1942

Kindly sponsored by HGC Peter Hewitt

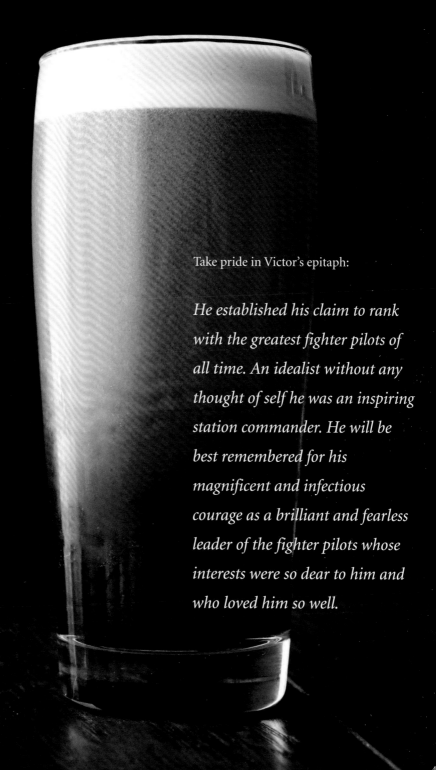

Take pride in Victor's epitaph:

He established his claim to rank with the greatest fighter pilots of all time. An idealist without any thought of self he was an inspiring station commander. He will be best remembered for his magnificent and infectious courage as a brilliant and fearless leader of the fighter pilots whose interests were so dear to him and who loved him so well.

It wasn't carrots. It was radar that gave him the edge, but this may improve your aim after midnight

Cat's Eyes Cunningham

John Cunningham was a night fighter ace. In a piece
of wartime propaganda to hide the invention of
airborne radar and to encourage the consumption of
carrots, the media was told his victories were simply a
result of being able to see in the dark. Flying
Blenheim and later Beaufighter night fighters from
RAF Middle Wallop, with his trusted radar operator,
Jimmy Rawnsley, he destroyed more than a dozen
enemy aircraft in single combat.

Ingredients

2 parts Guinness
1 part Ginger ale
1 part Lagavulin whisky

Born, tried, tested at *The Old Pack Horse* in
Chiswick by Bruce Dickinson. Further testing will
always improve stability one way or the other.

High Sheriffs' St Clement Cocktail

Since Saxon times, the shires of England and Wales have been blessed with a 'Shire Reeve'. The term led to Sheriffs, who became overly powerful (Nottingham and Robin Hood) and were reformed by Magna Carta. Now refashioned into the High Sheriff, it is an annual Royal Appointment. Both by law and practice the 55 High Sheriffs of England and Wales support the judiciary and all those who maintain The King's Peace, as well as their whole county much more broadly, with no expense falling on the public purse. It is a wonderful, historical reminder that not everything needs to be political.

Ingredients

8 parts High Sheriff's Gin
2 parts fresh juice of Amalfi lemons
1 part Cointreau

Method

Stir well, pour onto very cold ice, decorated with half a slice of orange and half of lemon and top up with chilled ginger ale to taste. Consume at once after raising the glass to St. Clement Danes and the Royal Air Force ideally to the sound of church bells or a passing Typhoon.

*On snowy days in more mountainous shires, High Sheriffs may prefer Brandy and Grand Marnier to Gin and Cointreau; in heatwaves in lowland shires they may find greater refreshment from more Cointreau and soda water rather than ginger ale.

128 Piccadilly Martini

The Royal Air Force Club at 128 Piccadilly is a national treasure. It was formed in 1919 and has been serving the Royal Air Force ever since. Situated in the heart of the West End it is only right and proper that it should have its own gin – 128 Piccadilly – and therefore its own cocktail – strangely enough called: 128 Piccadilly Martini.

The 128 Piccadilly gin is a London gin of superior quality and to make the martini, a London vermouth should be added in the ratio 2:1. The recommended vermouth is London Vermouth Company's No.3 SE Dry which is made with apples, gooseberries and honey. Therefore, a touch of apple brandy doesn't go amiss and a slice of apple garnishes this delightful 'sharpener' before dinner at the Club – or anywhere else where the Royal Air Force matters.

Kindly sponsored by the Trustees and Executive Team of the RAF Club

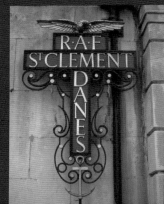

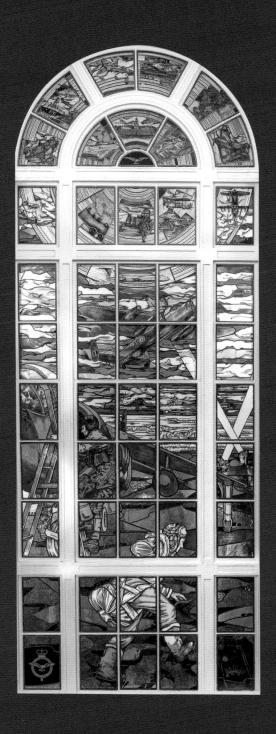

Flamboyance

There has been a tradition of the military for decades: picking collective nouns for certain ranks. For the British Army, the classic collective is that a gathering of Majors is called an ambition. So what, you may ask is a collection of three female Tornado pilots called? Simple. It's a flamboyance, hence this fizzing, sparkling and sometimes fruity cocktail.

Ingredients

3 measures 128 Piccadilly premium gin from the RAF Club
3 drops of Fee Brothers' chocolate bitters
1 measure Gabriel Boudier *crème de mures sauvages*
RAF Club house Champagne

Method

Take a tall Champagne flute and add three drops of chocolate bitters; then carefully add some crème de mure, followed by 3 measures of 128 Piccadilly premium gin and then top up with Champagne.

Sponsored by Jo Salter, Mandy Hickson
and Kirsty Murphy

The Merlin

Arguably the most famous piston-engine in the world, the Rolls-Royce Merlin powered the Hurricane, Lancaster, Mosquito and Spitfire to victory in the Second World War. What is not so well known is the origins of the Merlin, coming in a direct line from world-beating Schneider Trophy designs of Supermarine's RJ Mitchell.

Working hand-in-glove with Sir Henry Royce, Mitchell created designs which, in the hands of the Royal Air Force High Speed Flight, took the world speed record from 200 mph to over 400 mph. It was this shared dream of speed which pushed the boundaries of known aeronautical engineering with the Rolls-Royce PV12 inline engine.

The streamlined inline engine, which allowed Mitchell to reduce the airframe drag with a thinner fuselage, was world-beating at the time – 1929 and 1931 – allowing Britain to retain the Schneider Trophy in 1931. This cocktail has the smoothness of the powerplant, a streamlined taste and the kick of acceleration.

Ingredients

2 parts Chesterfield Dry Gin
1 part Londinio dry vermouth
1 part Italian vermouth
(Martini & Rosso dry)
4 drops of Bénédictine
Ice

Method

Fill a shaker with ice;
Add the two vermouths and stir;
Strain into a cocktail glass
To the shaker now add the gin and Bénédictine
Shake the gin for four minutes, strain into the glass
Consume and stand by to prepare a second

Kindly sponsored by Paul Beaver, Trustee, National Spitfire Project

Schneider Trophy programme 1931

Mosquito

The Volunteer

"An American citizen who died that England might live."

Billy Fiske

The archetypal British-American hero who was one of the first Americans to volunteer to fight against Nazi tyranny. He was a gold medallist in two Olympics and a Bentley Boy.

Ingredients

1 measure of vodka
1 measure of white rum
1 measure of silver tequila
1 measure of London gin
1 measure of triple sec
1 measure of simple syrup
1 measure fresh lemon juice
Cola
Lemon wedge garnish

Method

The spirits are added together in a tall ice-filled glass (a Collins glass in US parlance). Top up with a splash pf cola (or lemonade). Add the garnish and a reusable straw to sup.

Kindly sponsored by HGC Kevin Billings

Billy Fiske Passport

Flying Fortress

Forever linked to the bombing campaign against Germany in the Second World War, the Flying Fortress is also the poster-boy for the British and Commonwealth air operations in the North Atlantic. Found inadequate for the RAF Bomber Command's operations, it was a submarine killer. The Flying Fortress Cocktail remembers its roots in Northern Ireland and its successes.

Ingredients

1 part Irish whiskey
Berries from the bogs of Ireland (myrtle preferred)
2 parts Baileys Irish Cream
3 drops Fee Brothers' Cinnamon bitters
1 part Amaretto liquor for the bitterness of victory

Myrtle

Method

Take a cocktail shaker
Fill with ice and add four drops of cinnamon bitters
Add the whiskey – two jiggers should be fine
Shake vigorously
Add the Amaretto and top up with Baileys
Pour into a cocktail glass
Give thanks to Mr Boeing for such a strong aeroplane

Mr Boeing

Tempest

Three European nations are moving into the sixth generation of combat air systems – a whole system using the expertise of companies such as BAE Systems (UK), Leonardo (Italy) and Saab. It is the sixth generation, crewed or uncrewed and will be part of our defence until the middle of the century.

The Tempest cocktail goes above and beyond the normal. It can be prepared by anyone but drunk only be those ready to take the challenge.

fidante

Fidante Partners forms long-term alliances with talented investment teams to support and grow specialist investment management businesses.

Ingredients

Method

2 parts Swedish aquavit

2 parts London gin

3 parts Italian vermouth

Twist of fresh lemon

Cool a large cocktail glass with ice and rest in the freezer for 15 minutes – remove the glass and discard the ice

Carefully measure the ingredients and add a twist of lemon serve only to the discerning who understand the true value of the sixth generation.

Tempest goes above and beyond the normal

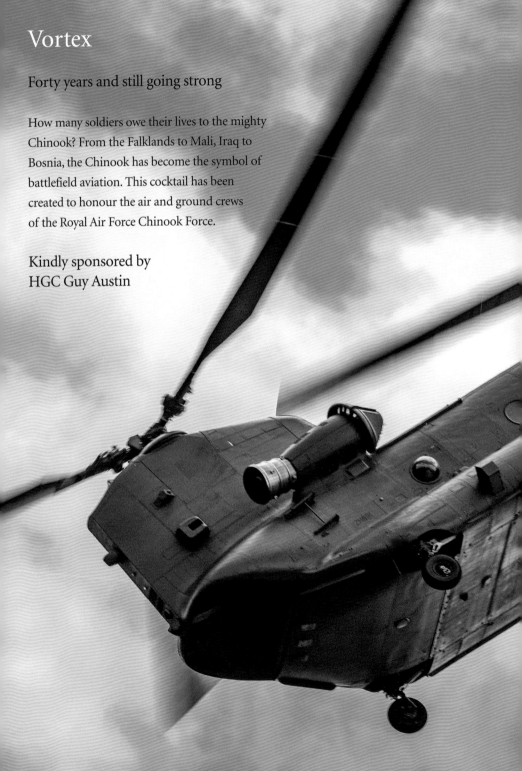

Vortex

Forty years and still going strong

How many soldiers owe their lives to the mighty
Chinook? From the Falklands to Mali, Iraq to
Bosnia, the Chinook has become the symbol of
battlefield aviation. This cocktail has been
created to honour the air and ground crews
of the Royal Air Force Chinook Force.

Kindly sponsored by
HGC Guy Austin

Ingredients

2 x shots of 128 Piccadilly Dry Gin
1 x shot of Mr Black Cold Brew coffee liqueur
Juice of half a lime

Method

Into a cold cocktail shaker, add plenty of ice and zest of
a lime, stir until very cold. Add the 128 Piccadilly gin,
then the black coffee liqueur and finally lime juice.

The Shadow

Hard at work but rarely seen, the Shadow is part of
the Nation's eyes and ears called ISR – Intelligence,
Surveillance and Reconnaissance. The Shadow is
based on the Beechcraft King Air 350 airframe
and extensively reworked by Raytheon in North
Wales. Proof of its utility is the 2021 contract for
more aircraft with improved equipment. They can't
come too soon as the world needs the Shadow's capabilities under the
capable management of No 14 Squadron at RAF Waddington.

Secret Ingredients

McQueen Black Cherry gin
Fevertree Light tonic
A sprig of fresh thyme

Tasting notes

An excellent combo with an excellent gin which
includes black cherries and vanilla to give a beautiful
red/purple hue. This is simple but delightful gin & tonic when served with a single ice cube.

The Shadow Method

This is simple even after a hard sortie close to the adversaries. A double shot of McQueen over
the ice and add as much tonic as one needs. The thyme sprig will probably be discarded for the
second sortie which will follow the first as quickly as one can say Vladimir Vladimirovich Putin.

Sponsored (by his family) in memory of Ken Allen who took early retirement from the RAF to
take up the post of Head Verger in 1975. He served the Church full time for 23 years and for
many more years in a part-time capacity after his "retirement". Ken was a keen photographer
and took many photographs of the Church which he freely gave to be used for postcards, sold in
aid of the Church.

One of St Clement Danes beautiful windows

The Spitfire

The Supermarine Spitfire needs no introduction. It is the world's most iconic fighter aeroplane. It is Hampshire's aeroplane too – designed, built, test flown and initially manufactured at Southampton. It is the fighter which helped save Britain, the Commonwealth and the Free World in 1940 in the Battle of Britain – without it the Battle could not have been won. To recognise Hampshire's role, the ingredients come from Hampshire locations.

Ingredients

Goodworth Sparkling Wine from Goodworth Clatford
2 parts Twisted Nose Gin from Winchester
1 part Churchwarden Apple Brandy from Kimpton

Method

This is a stirred cocktail which requires a good deep mixing bowl and glass mixer-rod. Add a generous three shots of gin and a single shot of brandy per person. Stir until a creamy colour and top up with the sparkling wine, remembering to try a drop 'naked' before you mix. Serve in a tall Champagne flute.

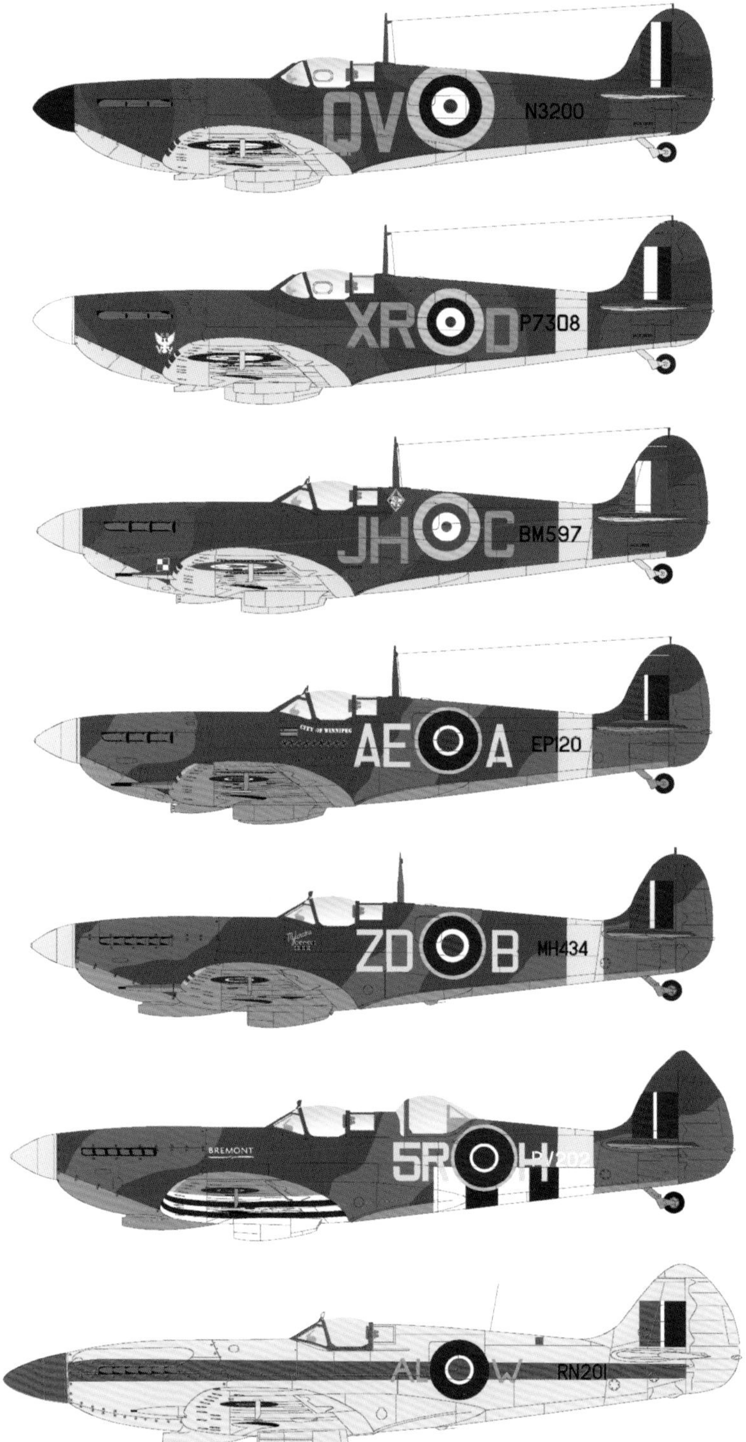

QV N3200

XR D P7308

JH C BM597

AE A EP120

ZD B MH434

5R H

A W RN201

Spitfire drawings by Jon Freeman, Taken from *Spitfire Evolution*

The Peto

Laura Sanderson writes: My grandfather, Acting Squadron Leader Charles 'Peto' Bennett OBE RAFVR saw distinguished service as a radar specialist during the Second World War. He was a talented engineer who was involved in the development of "Window" which was used in Operations TAXABLE and GLIMMER to support the D Day landings.

An Anglo-Norwegian, he subsequently took the capitulation of the German forces in Norway on behalf of the Royal Air Force.

He was a very stylish chap who had his service dress tailored on Jermyn Street and drank frequently enough at the Savoy to have his own cocktail created for him - the Peto, in the Savoy Cocktail Book.

Ingredients & Method

Add in order
The juice of a quarter orange
1 shot French vermouth (Lillet Blanc)
1 shot Italian vermouth (Martini & Rosso)
2 shots Plymouth gin
2 dashes Maraschino
Shake

The inclusion of Plymouth gin is significant- Peto was also a keen sailor who organised the sailing competition in the London post war Olympics of 1948.

Kindly sponsored by
Laura Sanderson in honour of her grandfather, Peto.

Peto and the rest of the Allied Military Commission taking the surrender from German officers in Norway on May 8th 1945

Lancaster Bomber

Perhaps the greatest aperitif ever created. A variant of the Negroni developed to perfection by the late Ian Lancaster, a member of the Diplomatic Corps who always needed a strong aperitif, hence it was named the 'Lancaster Bomber' in his memory.

The original Negroni is claimed by Italy and France. We won't delve too deeply except to say that Général Pascal Olivier de Negroni was a French cavalry officer who served in Senegal in 1857. This is a possible birthplace for this amazing cocktail. Others say he requested gin in place of soda water in his Americano in Florence in 1919, where the barman also swapped an orange slice for the usual lemon.

There are those who say it was discovered by the legendary Orson Welles in Rome in 1947. We know that a ready-made version has been on sale for more than a hundred years in Florence so that rules out Mr Welles. He did, however, do much to promote this delightful cocktail. You might ask, does it really matter who invented it? It certainly doesn't to my mind.

Ingredients

Two parts London Dry Gin or Downton Explorer
One part Campari bitters
One part Martini & Rossi Rosso

Method

No need for a cocktail shaker, but an old-fashioned glass
Fill it with ice and add Campari and Martini Rosso, stir
Add two jiggers of gin
Top up with soda for the second round
Garnish with an orange slice if you must

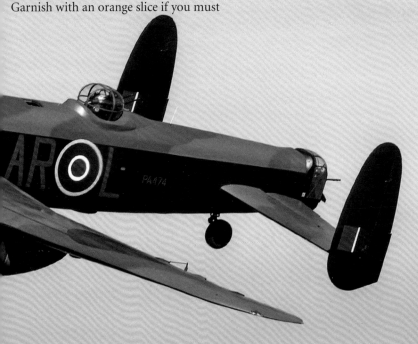

Magic

It is magic. No wonder the E-3 Sentry airborne warning and control aircraft has that call-sign. Being able to look across more than 200 nautical miles of airspace and create a 3D picture of that airspace is impressive. Now the E-3 is passing from the Royal Air Force inventory to be replaced by the E-7 Wedgetail which takes a technology jump of several decades. To maintain the British edge in air supremacy, the nation needs this immediate technology injection. The E-7 will be based alongside the P-8 Poseidon at RAF Lossiemouth, home too, to one of the nation's Typhoon QRA forces. The Magic cocktail needs to be powerful, subtle and have a secret ingredient.

Ingredients

3 shots of Speyside whisky
1 shot of ginger wine
Juice of a fresh lime
1 shot of the secret ingredient

Don't forget the secret ingredient, the Magic Circle forbids us to say what it is.

Method

Take a glass mixing bowl and add the ingredients, staring with the lime juice. Stir in each subsequent ingredient and then add the secret ingredient.

A Royal Air Force E-3D Sentry

Typhoon

This is the modern day Spitfire. It is the product of clever people in four countries working together to create the best twin-engined swing-role combat jet of its generation.

Typhoon will remain the United Kingdom's primary air defence fighter for another 20 years and by spiral integration, soon have a new radar advancing it half a generation.

To create the Typhoon cocktail is challenging as it needs to be able to swing from bitter to sweet, and dry to long. That means champagne is a must and that gin is a good base. This cocktail therefore has alternative ingredients depending on the drinker's mood. The basics give a distinct nod to Lancashire, the home of Warton and Samesbury factories.

Ingredients

Champagne
Lancashire Signature London Dry Gin
Raisthorpe Rhubarb in liqueur
Red Rose water for Lancashire
Bitters to taste

Method

Take a cold shaker, add ice and the gin and the rhubarb in equal measures. Use Angostura bitters for a dry, bitter taste or rose water for a sweeter experience. Whatever happens, top up with champagne. The choice is yours.

Kindly sponsored by beam earth

b e a m

The extensive and deep-rooted experience in environmental and positive impact approach across investing, pension fund management, energy and natural resource industries, gives our multi-talented teams a unique edge, and the ability to cross fertilise their knowledge and skills, adding value from different points of view to each business line.

Blenheim Bellini

Every visitor to Venice knows about Harry's Bar near the Grand Canal on Sestiere San Marco. Every visitor should also have sampled the amazing Bellini invented in the Second World War by Giuseppe Cipriani, the founder of the bar. It is said that the colour created mixing white peach nectar with an Italian sparkling, reminded him of the colour of a Bellini masterpiece's saint's robes.

No. 601 Squadron has gone step further, changed the prosecco for Franciacorta La Sparviere Brut Cuvée N.7 and added peach brandy to give the cocktail a kick – like pushing boost on a Spitfire's Merlin engine.

Is there an aviation connection? Not really, but best not consume before flight.

Ingredients

3 shots of white peach nectar
2 shots of peach brandy
6 shots of Franciacorta
1 slice of fresh white peach

Method

It is important to keep the ratio 2:1 for the sparkling wine and the nectar but the brandy is negotiable! It can be made at home with vodka and fresh peaches plus a vanilla pod. It needs the vanilla to counter some of the peach sweetness.

Take a champagne flute, add the peach brandy then the nectar, top up with Franciacorta and add the peach slice after first running it around the rim of the glass.

Kindly sponsored by
Ian Williams in honour of his father, Brian.

Sporty Spice
Sponsored by the RAF Central Fund

Not every cocktail has to be alcoholic. Some can be made to taste just as exciting using standard ingredients. An example is the Sporty Spice, especially created for this book as an example of what can be done.

Your RAF Charity for
Sport & Physical Activities

We want everyone in the RAF regardless of their role, rank, physical ability or competing level to have access to sports facilities, equipment, and training through our support we help to safeguard their health and wellbeing.

Ingredients

3 shots of Monin coffee syrup
(Monin salted caramel is an interesting alternative)
1 portion of whipped cream (to taste)
2 shots of Monin gingerbread syrup
A dash of lemon juice
A dash of orange juice

(to make your own coffee syrup add a cup of instant coffee granules or coffee from a Nespresso machine (other brands exist I'm told), add a little caster sugar, heat and then reduce to ensure the taste is powerful enough to keep the Coningsby QRA awake. To make the ginger syrup, add ground ginger to golden caster sugar and about 200 ml of water, boil and reduce)

Method

To an ice cold shaker, add coffee and ginger syrups and shake well. Pour into a standard glass and top up with the whipped cream. Then, to remember St Clement Danes, add a couple of dashes of oranges and lemons (say the bells of St Clement's) to kick the mocktail into life. It's a real teaser because few will know its not a vodka or brandy cocktail. Smug and sober.

Pablo's Last Stand

Designed with Pablo - who I hear has flown a few aeroplanes in his time - in mind; this drink may look perfectly innocent to those to whom it's served but be warned there is hidden depth, experience and potential lethality. This elixir, which deserves true respect, must be approached with stealth and has proven itself as the most worthy ally to accompany the cheese board at the end of the evening: ditch the port. Let's be frank, a fuller, lined stomach to accompany this devilish drink should be advised, for everyone's sake. Take heart however, this 'Last Stand' drink will ensure you're well preserved if you succeed in falling over at the end of the night.

Kindly sponsored by No 601 for their long-standing PMC's last stand.

To take part in the journey of the 'Last Stand', combine:

2 parts Armagnac, for that trusted base
1 part Cointreau, or triple sec if you wish
1 part Crème de Cassis, flying in memories of Les Landes
1 part Southern Comfort, crossing over to the Sunshine State
½ part Chili Honey Vodka, providing that kick from the old USSR
1 part lemon, tying it off with a Levantine twist

Shake well, pour into an ice cold glass, and enjoy. Good luck and do wait a few hours before taking up the controls.

by Eloise Coombs.

Padre's Punch

Resident Chaplain's Cocktail

Everyone needs guidance once in a while. Royal Air Force Commissioned Chaplains provide pastoral and spiritual care for all personnel and their dependants irrespective of religious belief or status - a valuable source of personal well-being and guidance in times of war and peace. They affirm the unique value and worth of every human being and are dedicated to celebrating the diversity that marks our world.

The chaplains of the Royal Air Force are committed to an all souls ministry, which makes no distinction on the grounds of race, religion, age, disability, gender, sexual orientation or gender identity. Members of the Service can always call on the Resident Chaplain at St Clement Danes, the Central Church of the Royal Air Force.

Reverend Mark Perry, the current Chaplain began his tenure in May 2022 with the words: "Being a chaplain in the Royal Air Force is a privilege. I serve extraordinary people, not least the Whole Force community from St Clement Danes and all that this beautiful Wren Church offers to the diverse family of the Royal Air Force. The Church's history is something to behold and has an exciting future ahead."

To help with the challenges coming up, the following punch has been devised to combine oranges (well, tangerines) and lemon (and limes) with a Biblical theme of cinnamon, honey and a clove.

Padre Mark with SCD Ambassadors Hon Gp Capts Sally Bridgeland & Paul Beaver

Ingredients

Freshly squeezed tangerine juice
Freshly squeezed lime juice
Freshly squeezed lemon juice
Teaspoon of liquid honey
4 x cinnamon sticks
A single clove
Mineral water

Method

This is a punch. Think big, go big. Using a large punch bowl, simply add the ingredients. Stir well and ladle the punch into cups and serve, in abundance, of course.

Editor's note: goes well with Tequila
if required, and in moderation

Churchill Special

As Winston Churchill said he was 'easily satisfied by the best', we have created a cocktail which reflects some of the best ingredients available in any bar or home. Winston is best known for his liking of Pol Roger, fino sherry, bourbon and Grand Marnier orange brandy. So why not combine them? The trick is combining in the right measures.

Ingredients

2 measures of Woodford bourbon
1 measure of Dry Sack dry sherry
1.5 measures of Grand Marnier
An appropriate amount of
Pol Roger NV or premium cyder

Method

This is a cocktail which requires to be prepared cold and served with ice. Depending on the side of the Atlantic, the ice added at the end will vary, remembering that ice is sometimes the enemy of a good cocktail (unless it is drunk with vitesse).

Add the sherry to the bourbon, then the Grand Marnier. Stir the spirits until well mixed and then top with champagne. To be honest Pol Roger might be wasted in a spirit-based cocktail, so it could be taken as a chaser. Perhaps try instead The Winston 2018 from The Newt in Somerset, a relatively new sparking cyder maker in the traditional style which, of course, led to the champagne method of double fermentation.

Kindly sponsored by HGC Sally Bridgeland

St Clement Danes Cocktails Tick List PLEASE DRINK WISELY

The connoisseur will want to try each and every cocktail in this collection. To make this process easier and to encourage careful consumption, we have a list, a tick box and a date of first trial.

	Pages	Tick	Date		Pages	Tick	Date
Ukrainian Flag Cocktail	7			Cat's Eyes Cunningham	48/49		
St Clement Danes Cocktail	8/9			High Sheriffs' Cocktail	50/51		
St Clement Danes Martini	10/11			128 Piccadilly Martini	52/53		
Pablo's Margarita	12/13			Flamboyance	54/55		
Flying Sword	14/15			The Merlin	56/57		
French 75 (mod)	16/17			The Volunteer	58/59		
The Special Relationship	18/19			Flying Fortress	60/61		
Actuary's Angel	20/21			Tempest	62/63		
Forces Mutual Mojito	22/23			Vortex	64/65		
Flaming Hot	24/25			The Shadow	66/67		
No 601 Champagne Cocktail	26/27			The Spitfire	68/69		
The Investor's Return	28/29			The Peto	70/71		
Black Buck	30/31			Lancaster Bomber	72/73		
Champagne Claudia	32/33			Magic	74/75		
St Clement Old Fashioned	34/35			Typhoon	76/77		
Rigby Pathfinder	36/37			Blenheim Bellini	78/79		
Hitomi Blitz	38/39			Sporty Spice	80/81		
Catalina	40/41			Pablo's Last Stand	82/83		
Defiant	42/43			Padre's Punch	84/85		
Blue & White	44/45			Churchill Special	86/87		
The Beamish	46/47